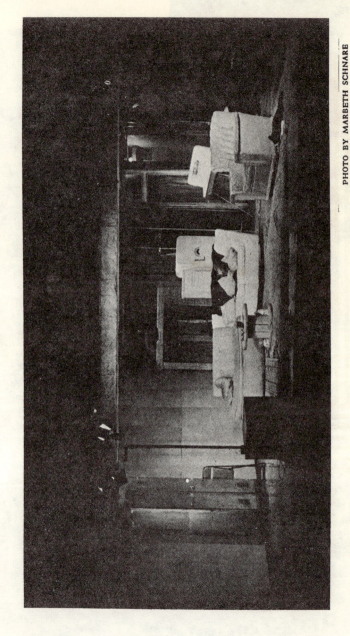

Set for the New York production of "Say Goodnight, Gracie." Designed by Jack Chandler.

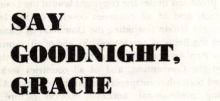

SAY GOODNIGHT, GRACIE

BY

RALPH PAPE

**DRAMATISTS
PLAY SERVICE
INC.**

SOUND EFFECTS RECORD

The following sound effects record, which may be used in con-
nection with production of this play, can be obtained from
Thomas J. Valentino, Inc., 151 West 46th Street, New York,
N. Y. 10036.

No. 5025—Telephone ring, doorbell

For Austin

SAY GOODNIGHT, GRACIE opened Off-Broadway at the Actors' Playhouse on July 6, 1979. It was directed by Austin Pendleton, and the set was by Jack Chandler, costumes by Patricia Wiegleb and lighting by Cheryl Thacker. The producers were Wayne Adams and Douglas Urbanski. The associate producer was Willard Morgan; production stage manager, Amy Whitman.

The cast in order of appearance was:

JERRY .... Tom McKitterick
STEVE .... Mark Blum
GINNY .... Molly Regan
BOBBY .... Danton Stone
CATHERINE .... Carolyn Groves

SAY GOODNIGHT, GRACIE was first developed in a workshop production at Playwrights Horizons, New York City, in November, 1978, under the direction of Austin Pendleton; Robert Moss, Producing Director. It later opened in February, 1979 at the 78th St. Theatre, New York City, under the direction of Austin Pendleton, on a mini-contract, and ran for 117 performances with the following cast:

JERRY .... Willard Morgan
STEVE .... Mark Blum
GINNY .... Molly Regan
BOBBY .... Danton Stone
CATHERINE .... Carolyn Groves

The producers were Wayne Adams and Douglas Urbanski

P<small>LACE</small>: The apartment shared by Jerry and Ginny in the East Village, N.Y.C.

<h2 style="text-align:center">CHARACTERS</h2>

S<small>TEVE</small>, a writer.
J<small>ERRY</small>, an actor.
G<small>INNY</small>, a secretary.
B<small>OBBY</small>, a rock-and-roll singer.
C<small>ATHERINE</small>, an airline stewardess.

All characters are in their late 20s.

SAY GOODNIGHT, GRACIE

It is late September, about 5:30 in the evening. The interior of Jerry and Ginny's apartment in the East Village. There is a couch in the middle of the room; a couple of folding chairs piled in the corner; a small coffee table; an old TV (the older the better) pushed out of the way in a corner; possibly a couple of posters on the walls. Upstage Center is the kitchen area. A small refrigerator can be seen. To the Left of this, a bathtub and a rather beat-up-looking sink (plumbing fixtures included) are also visible. Further Upstage Left is the entrance to the apartment. Upstage Right is the bedroom area; bunkbeds are seen through the doorway. There can also be a curtained-off area for changing clothes. Downstage Right is Jerry's locker. Downstage Left is an old upholstered chair.

Upstage Left, a door opens and closes. Jerry enters. He has a traveling bag over his shoulder. He is carrying an 8 × 10 glossy of himself. There are a few moments of indecisive action. At last, he sits on the couch, stares at his picture and tears it up.

JERRY. What next?

STEVE. (*He has been hiding behind the sofa. Quietly, he appears. He is wearing a gorilla mask and a brown derby. Jerry has not seen him.*) Excuse me, do you know what time it is?

JERRY. Holy shit!

STEVE. Wait. Before you say anything. I've got something wonderful to tell you! (*He removes mask as he speaks.*)

JERRY. WHAT ARE YOU DOING IN MY APARTMENT?! You trying to give me a heart attack or something?!

STEVE. Oh, it's OK, Ginny let me in. She went to pick up her dress at the cleaners. How'd the audition go?

JERRY. What are you doing in my apartment, Steve?!

STEVE. You weren't right for the part, were you?

JERRY. Never mind! (*Jerry moves to kitchen area.*)

STEVE. Jerry, it doesn't *matter!* Wait till you hear what—

7

JERRY. Not now! Please.

STEVE. Oh boy! Just wait till you hear what I've got to tell you! Come on: ask me what it is. I haven't told *anybody* yet—Ginny'll be right back, Bobby'll be here, we'll be leaving for the reunion—Come on!

JERRY. (*Turning around; holding an empty pot by the handle.*) Where's the Chunky Turkey soup?

STEVE. Soup? Soup? Who cares about soup?

JERRY. Where's the Chunky Turkey soup?

STEVE. I ate it! It was delicious! I thank you from the bottom of my heart!

JERRY. You ate the Chunky Turkey soup?

STEVE. Yes! I was all alone, I was excited and hungry and I wanted to celebrate and here was this little can crying out: Take me, open me, eat me, I'm yours!

JERRY. In *my* cabinet, Steve, in *my* kitchen, in *my* apartment, there are the following items—

STEVE. And do you know *why* I was so excited???

JERRY. —3 cans of Chunky Beef soup, 3 cans of Chunky Vegetable soup, 3 cans of Chunky Split Pea and Ham soup, and 7 family-size cans of Franco-American Spaghettios. Are you listening?

STEVE. What are you doing? (*Almost immediately.*) Rehearsing a monologue! (*He watches and listens to Jerry.*)

JERRY. Early this morning, as I was about to leave *my* apartment, I paused for a moment in *my* kitchen and looked in *my* cabinet, and I made certain that hidden away behind all those other items, there was still one remaining can of Chunky Turkey soup. Why did I do this?

STEVE. (*Checking imaginary watch.*) 10 . . . 9 . . . 8 . . .

JERRY. I did this because Chunky Turkey soup, as you know, for some mysterious reason, has become almost impossible to locate in this part of the city, and because I like it very much. In fact, I love it! Why do I love it? I don't know. I can't honestly tell you why I love Chunky Turkey soup. All I know is—

STEVE. Hey, thanks *so* much for coming. We would have preferred hearing something from Shakespeare, but this gives us a damn fine idea of your talents, and believe me, if a part *should* turn up—

JERRY. All I know is: I love it! It is dependable. It is there. It is the last thing I can be certain of in a world filled with uncertainty; and

8

in any case I don't believe that an emotion such as love has to be explained. Do you agree?

STEVE. Are you all right?

JERRY. *Do* you agree?

STEVE. My God, it was only a can of soup!

JERRY. It was only a can of soup. Was that what you said?

STEVE. Yes.

JERRY. Guess what word you left out?

STEVE. I have no idea.

JERRY. Guess.

STEVE. I don't know!

JERRY. Take a guess!

STEVE. But I don't know!

JERRY. What's the word?!

STEVE. (*As Groucho.*) Hmmn. It wouldn't be "swordfish," would it?

JERRY. My! The word is "my." My, my, my, my, my! It was only *my* fucking can of soup!

STEVE. You are really angry.

JERRY. Oh, yeah? How can you tell? Seriously. As an actor, it's important that I be able to recognize such things. Come on. How can you be sure I'm angry?

STEVE. All right. Put down the pot.

JERRY. You want me to put down the pot? OK. I'll put down the pot, Steve. Oh, I'll put *down* the pot! Are you sure you *really* want to see me put down the pot??

STEVE. Oh, stop it. You sound just like Jackie Gleason!!

JERRY. DON'T YOU EVER TELL ME I SOUND LIKE JACKIE GLEASON!!

STEVE. I'm sorry. That was the wrong thing to say.

JERRY. Don't you *ever* say that again!

STEVE. I'm sorry.

JERRY. Now I've got a headache.

STEVE. It's my fault.

JERRY. I know it's your fault.

STEVE. I said—

JERRY. Don't say another word!

STEVE. But— (*Jerry sits down on couch.*)

JERRY. Don't say another word! (*Closes his eyes.*) I've got to relax. Dear God, I've got to relax. Don't say another word. Just let me relax . . .

9

STEVE. May I make an observation? Do you know why you have so much trouble at auditions? It's because you're tense. It's very hard to feel at ease in the presence of someone who's unnaturally tense. Do you know what your body says to the average person? It says: Tension. Do you realize what the—

JERRY. Why don't you ever listen to me?

STEVE. Because I'm your friend. What's the matter? Did your boss give you more static about taking off to go to auditions?

JERRY. Can't you see I've got a lot on my mind? And it's more than just an audition or a job that's bothering me?

STEVE. Of course I can see that. I'm not insensitive. Will you just let me tell you what I've been trying to tell you?

JERRY. Would you like a beer?

STEVE. Sure. Fine. (*Jerry gets the beer, hands one to Steve.*) Thanks. OK. Are you ready for this? You know that girl with the red hair who comes in the book store where I work? Miriam? Well, she knows I'm a writer, and she said she didn't know why she never thought of it before, but this morning she tells me if I ever come up with an outline for a situation comedy pilot, she has got contacts with Norman Lear and can get him to read it! Do you believe this?! Norman Lear?! Producer of *All in the Family; Mary Hartman, Mary Hartman;* right? OK. *Now.* By a strange coincidence, what do you suppose I have been working on in secret for the past two months? A completely original TV series in which—now, hold on to your seat!—I have modelled the central character on you. I even gave him your name! His name is Jerry! One day it just comes to me: a situation comedy about a group of people who are members of the very *first* TV generation, born and raised during the dawn of the Atomic Age, whose lives have gone nowhere, whose dreams have been shattered, who see themselves as hopeless failures, or, at best, historical curiosities, and who do not have the slightest idea what to do about it! I mean: I firmly believe the time is ripe for something like this: it cannot miss! Do you see what I'm getting at? You'll never have to work in an office again. When the show is picked up, guess who I'm going to recommend for the part? There will be no way they can turn you down! Well? What do you think? (*Pause.*)

JERRY. Steve, I hate to tell you this.

STEVE. Tell me what?

JERRY. You're fantasizing again.

STEVE. No, no, no! I'm not fantasizing again. You're wrong!

10

What I'm writing now is the cumulative result of everything that has happened to me in the last ten years: this is it! I know it! OK, OK, so maybe it sounds a little pretentious, but I'm convinced that I have finally achieved some form of maturity as an artist.

JERRY. (*Holding up gorilla mask.*) Maturity, Steve?

STEVE. Don't you appreciate what I'm trying to do for you? I was trying to cheer you up. I thought it would make you laugh!

JERRY. It was a great success, Steve. Thank you.

STEVE. (*Taking mask quickly.*) Hey, don't tell me you don't remember this? I found it in a box in my closet last week. You used to have one, too. Don't you remember in grammar school we used to watch the Ernie Kovacs Show over at Bobby's house, and there was this routine called The Nairobi Trio with these guys in gorilla suits, so the three of us went out and bought these masks and we used to get all dressed up every—

JERRY. Steve, we're almost 30 years old!

STEVE. So what!

JERRY. You know why I feel sorry for you?

STEVE. You know I do. (*Pause.*) It's been 15 years since Ambrose died, but to me he was always more than just a parakeet. . . .

JERRY. Because you're silly! Let's face it, *you are a silly man.* There's no other word for it. I, on the other hand, am a stupid man. But you know what? I would *rather* be a stupid man than a silly man, because a stupid man at least *tries,* a stupid man *cares,* a stupid man, in his own *stupid* way, has integrity! Not like a silly man! How can a silly man *care* about anything, or *have* integrity, or—or—

STEVE. Don't stop now. This is much better than the speech about the soup.

JERRY. Goddammit, Steve! Does it amuse you to watch my mind turning into a piece of Swiss cheese? Well, does it? (*From L., Ginny enters, wearing her office clothes. She is carrying a dress on a hanger. The dress is covered with a plastic bag from the cleaners.*)

GINNY. Hello, hello, hello, hello, hello.

STEVE. Hi, Ginny.

GINNY. (*To Jerry.*) Hi, like my hair? Mr. Norris let me have the afternoon off so I could go have it done. How was the audition? (*Pause.*) You weren't right for the part, were you? What did the director say? I bet he said you gave the best audition he saw all week.

JERRY. He said this character in the play needed to convince the

11

audience he possessed certain qualities, and that unfortunately they were all qualities he didn't think I could convey.

GINNY. Like what?

JERRY. Maturity, strength, belief in his ultimate worth as a human being—shall I go on?

GINNY. That's ridiculous! Didn't he look at your resumé? I mean, you did all those Shakespeare and Greek things—and you even played what's-his-name in college.

JERRY. Who do you mean?

GINNY. You know who I mean.

JERRY. Who?

GINNY. You know—what's-his-name?

JERRY. Hamlet?

GINNY. Hamlet! That's who I mean. You even played Hamlet in college. Didn't he see that?

JERRY. He implied I would be wise to delete that as well as several other items from my resumé! He told me to walk over to this mirror and look into it, and then he asked me if I honestly thought I could see Hamlet in that mirror. I said, yes, I could. "No, Jerry," he said, "you only *think* you see Hamlet in that mirror. What you really see in that mirror is the face of a man terrified of his own toothbrush. The face of a man so afraid to leave his home he thinks the ground will open up and swallow him if he steps outside." Those were his exact words.

GINNY. Jerry.

JERRY. Then, as I was about to leave, he shook my hand and smiled and he said the one word that is the most encouraging word you can hear after an audition. He said: "Wait." (*Pause.*) He said, "Look, I like you and I respect you, and because of that respect, which I hope is mutual, I feel an obligation to be completely frank with you at this moment, Jerry. Always remember. *You* are never going to play Hamlet on a professional stage. *You* are never going to play Macbeth. *You* are never going to play King Lear . . . Never. Never. Never. Never. Never . . . but thank you for coming."

GINNY. Don't take it personally.

STEVE. Ginny, *I* think your hair looks beautiful.

GINNY. Why thank you, Stephen. Now, I hope I didn't hear the two of you arguing before I came in.

STEVE. If you hadn't shown up, I'd probably be a bloody pulp by now—it all started because I told Jerry I had a surprise for him.

12

GINNY. What's that?

STEVE. I'm writing a pilot for a situation comedy that's going to be read by Norman Lear, and when it's picked up, I'm going to arrange for Jerry to star in it.

GINNY. That's wonderful! Oh, that's really wonderful, Stephen. Isn't that wonderful, Jerry?

STEVE. Jerry said he didn't want me to make him famous. He said he enjoyed being miserable. Then he slapped me around for about fifteen minutes, and holding a knife to my throat, he swore that if I ever tried to bring a little sunshine into his life again, he would kill me.

GINNY. (*Paying him no mind, she heads for the bedroom.*) That's nice. Listen, I've just *got* to get out of these clothes.

STEVE. Pick out something nice for Jerry to wear to the—

JERRY. (*Cutting him off—the following exchange is "whispered."*) Steve, before you say any more—I'm not going to the reunion tonight.

STEVE. What? You're kidding, right?

JERRY. Will you take Ginny for me? The two of you will be with Bobby and whoever he's got for a girl friend these days. It'll be like a double date for her.

STEVE. (*Loudly—for Ginny's benefit.*) How about those Mets? (*Back to Jerry.*) You're not going to the reunion?

JERRY. I just can't go. OK? I just can't. I need one night by myself to do some thinking. Will you take her for me?

STEVE. But the only reason she wants to go to this reunion is because of you!

JERRY. I know, I know. I just wish she'd think of herself for a change. I tried to tell you that, but—I just can't talk to her anymore. She doesn't hear me, or something.

STEVE. Well, you're not exactly the easiest person in the world to talk to, you know.

JERRY. And do you know that some of the people she works with think we're married? And she hasn't bothered to tell them the truth?

STEVE. (*Loudly—for Ginny's benefit.*) Great double play combination! (*To Jerry.*) Ah, you should've seen her before—she's so excited and nervous about tonight, she was spinning like a top, her eyes were like two little lights—

JERRY. I don't want to hear this—

STEVE. —why, she told me that she hasn't been so excited since the night you and she met . . . when she opened the door

13

. . . and saw you there . . . for the first time . . . asleep in that basket, clutching your picture and resume and that little hand-written note that made her cry as she read it aloud: "Please give this man a home. His needs are very simple: Food. Shelter. Clothing. A Weekly Allowance—"

JERRY. Why do you love to make up stories about me?

STEVE. Is this a story? Did you not tell me when you first met Ginny that you would never do anything to hurt her feelings?

JERRY. Dammit, I *don't* want to hurt her feelings—that's why I'm asking you to help me persuade her to go to the reunion without me—I need to be by myself tonight because there's a lot of things I have to think about, and my relationship with Ginny is one of them.

GINNY. Jerry, I'm going to hang out your Oxford blue shirt for tonight. Is that OK? (*Pause.*) I said: is that OK?

STEVE. Why yes, dear, that would be just fine. And would you see if you could possibly locate my cordovan wingtips while you're back there? And that floral ascot—you know the one, don't you dear? —the one with the embroidered initials?

GINNY. (*Laughing.*) Oh, stop it, Stephen. Jerry, is there another shirt you'd rather wear to the reunion? (*She comes out of the bedroom.*)

JERRY. Ginny, I'm not going to the reunion tonight.

GINNY. You're not going to the reunion? Oh my God, you can't be serious!

JERRY. I have to do my exercises. (*He gets a blanket and some exercise equipment out of the locker during the following exchange, spreads the blanket out on the floor and begins to do a variety of fairly strenuous calisthenics.*)

GINNY. You're really not going?!

JERRY. I don't want to talk about it. Look, I'm sorry. You'll just have to go with Steve.

GINNY. With Steve??? (*To Steve.*) No offense, Stephen.

STEVE. Please. That's what I'm here for.

GINNY. (*To Jerry.*) But why? Just because you had one terrible audition? You've had a thousand terrible auditions!

JERRY. It wasn't only the audition! It was a lot of things. Look, I'm sorry. I *know* I promised to go. You'll just have to believe me. The last thing I want to do tonight is confront my past. All right? Please understand that.

14

GINNY. But I don't want to go to New Jersey by myself! Besides, it's *your* reunion, not *mine!*

JERRY. You won't be by yourself. Don't worry. Steve will protect you. And you'll be with Bobby and his girl friend.

GINNY. And what in heaven's name are you going to tell Bobby? My God, you know how sensitive Bobby is! And he's cancelling a concert tonight and driving up all the way from Asbury Park, New Jersey—

STEVE. Probably stoned out of his mind.

GINNY. Probably stoned out of his mind. Just so he can drive his two oldest friends to their high school reunion, and now you're going to tell him you're not going? That's just the kind of thing that could push Bobby over the edge. How am I supposed to entertain your friends if you won't help me? Or don't you care if anyone feels welcome in our home anymore? (*Jerry continues to exercise.*) Answer me, Jerry! (*The phone rings.*) Oh shit! If that's Bobby, I will *not* know what to say to him! You had better answer that phone, Jerry. (*The phone rings.*) Jerry, would you stop pretending you can't hear me, and answer the phone! (*The phone rings.*) Jerry!

STEVE. Would you like me to answer the phone?

GINNY. Please, Stephen. Would you? (*Jerry continues to exercise.*)

STEVE. Hello? . . . Bobby? Yeah . . . *Where are you?* Uh-huh . . . no, number 115 . . . 3rd floor . . . uh-huh . . . uh-huh . . . what's her name? . . . uh-huh . . . well, yeah, Ginny's here . . . but she can't come to the phone . . . are you sitting down? Don't ask me why, just sit down . . . (*Steve takes a deep breath.*) He's dead . . . about 10 minutes ago . . . no, this is *not* a gag.

GINNY. *Stephen!*

STEVE. Got a heart attack doing those stupid exercises of his . . . fell right onto the coffee table . . . Ginny and I were sitting there, I was doing the crossword puzzle in TV Guide. We heard this moan . . . we looked up . . . I managed to pull the bowl of potato chips clear in time . . . it was terrible . . . I only needed one more word . . . not that that's important, of course . . . Bobby, why are you laughing? I don't think this is anything to laugh at, Bob. Wait, don't hang up, I'm not through—hello?

GINNY. Where was Bobby calling from?

STEVE. Downstairs on the corner. He forgot the number of the building.

GINNY. He's downstairs already!? He's not supposed to be here for another two hours! He mentioned his girl friend. What was he saying about his girl friend?

STEVE. Her name's Catherine. She's an airline stewardess. And they've been living together for almost a year.

GINNY. Her name is Catherine. She's an airline stewardess. And they've been living together for almost a year.

JERRY. Relax.

GINNY. Relax? How can I relax? Look, Jerry, I know you've got a lot on your mind, but I would hope you would consider *my* feelings once in a while.

JERRY. I am considering your feelings, Ginny.

GINNY. You are not. You *know* that I'm going to find it very difficult to go all the way out to that reunion without you. You *know* that . . . And what should I tell all the people you went to high school with when they want to know why the famous actor didn't show up?

JERRY. Tell them anything. Tell them what Steve told Bobby over the phone.

GINNY. Don't talk like that!

JERRY. It doesn't matter what you tell them.

GINNY. It does too matter! Don't you ever talk like that! The two of you open up these chairs—Stephen, cut that out! (*Steve has been mimicking Jerry doing his exercises and he continues to do so—the actress playing Ginny may need to ad lib some more orders to him during this scene, while she tries hurriedly to get the room in order.*) Jerry, fold up your blanket . . . please be nice to Bobby, no matter how you feel. He's your friend and we haven't seen him in over a year . . . (*The doorbell rings.*) I'm just glad I'm not the one who's going to have to break poor Bobby's heart. Stephen, will you please stop that?! Now, I'm not going to mention anything about your not going to the reunion. You're going to have to tell Bobby yourself. All right?

JERRY. All right.

STEVE. *All right!* (*The doorbell rings: Ginny goes to answer.*)

GINNY. Hi, Bobby. Come in, come in.

BOBBY. Hi, Ginny, how are ya? We got here early.

CATHERINE. Hello.

16

GINNY. Hi, you must be Catherine, I'm Ginny, come in, come in. (*All enter and come to* C.)

BOBBY. Hey, hey Jerry, baby!

JERRY. (*Weakly.*) Hi, Bobby.

BOBBY. What's the matter? Is somethin' wrong? (*To Ginny.*) Is somethin' wrong with Jerry?

GINNY. Oh no, just a—

JERRY. Headache. I still have a little headache.

GINNY. He still has a little headache.

BOBBY. Is that all? Well, fuck the headache. We can't have no headaches tonight, am I right?

JERRY. Right.

BOBBY. Better believe it! (*Pointing to Steve, who is "dramatically" feigning a headache.*) This guy better not have no headache—hey, Ginny, this guy got a headache, too?

GINNY. What? I'm sorry. What did you—?

BOBBY. (*Abruptly, to Ginny.*) You got a headache?

GINNY. Me? You mean me? (*Laughing.*) No, no, no, no, no, I don't have a—

BOBBY. (*Abruptly.*) How ya doin' Stevie?

STEVE. How ya doin', punk?

BOBBY. Terrific, man, terrific. Hey, this here is Catherine. Is she beautiful, or what? That's Jerry.

CATHERINE. Hello, Jerry. Nice to meet you.

JERRY. Hi.

BOBBY. And that's Stevie.

CATHERINE. Hello, Steve.

STEVE. Hello.

GINNY. And I'm Ginny.

CATHERINE. Yes. I remember.

GINNY. Oh right, I just told you my name at the door.

BOBBY. So! Tonight's the night. I love reunions.

GINNY. Hey, Bobby, you look wonderful! You get younger-looking every time we see you!

BOBBY. Why, thank you, Ginny. That means a lot to me, really.

GINNY. Well, it's true! Here, let me take your things. It's so early yet, I'm not even dressed, can I get you anything? Beer? Coffee? I just bought some of those continental coffees. They're really delicious, just like they say. Bobby, *you* would love the mocha flavor, I know you would. Can I make you a cup?

17

BOBBY. Mocha?

CATHERINE. It's like chocolate.

BOBBY. Oh.

GINNY. So what can I get you? Hmmmmmmmnn?

BOBBY. Ginny, believe it or not, we are stuffed.

CATHERINE. We just ate.

GINNY. Oh, I'm sorry to hear that. I mean I'm not sorry you *ate*. Was it good? Oh, I bet it was. I mean I'm sorry I can't—

CATHERINE. We understand.

GINNY. —get you something. And I can't offer you any smoke because—

CATHERINE. (*Indicating her purse.*) Oh, we have plenty of smoke with us.

GINNY. —Lloyd was out sick all this week. Oh, you do? Oh, well, that's great! Well, then there's no problem. Lloyd works in the mail room at our company, and deals a little on the side. He's been out sick.

CATHERINE. You're a secretary?

GINNY. Yes. Yes, I am.

CATHERINE. Bobby told me.

GINNY. I am. Yes.

CATHERINE. You like it?

GINNY. Oh, I love it. It's a big, beautiful office. All the people are really nice. And Mr. Norris says he would be absolutely *lost* without me!

CATHERINE. Your employer?

GINNY. Yes . . . Mr. Norris is my boss. God, it's going to be five years in January. Isn't that incredible? I mean how time just flies?

CATHERINE. "The Bird of Time Has But a Little Way to Flutter/And the Bird is on the Wing."

GINNY. Oh, I know, I know. Anyway Mr. Norris is *very* nice, a very nice man, in fact he's almost like a father to me, which is not to say he doesn't have these certain rules that he's extremely fussy about, like once, I mean I knew it was dumb, but I was going to be late and the Star-Lite was crowded, so I went to another deli and picked up coffee and a toasted bran muffin for him, and as soon as he bit into the muffin, he *knew* that it was not his regular muffin and he gave me this look, right? Well, I felt just awful, I could see he was so disappointed in me— (*Steve feigns breaking down in tears— Ginny hurries to the end of her story.*) but he's really very sweet and I

18

know he really meant it when he said he would be absolutely lost without me, you're a stewardess?

CATHERINE. Yes.

GINNY. That must be exciting, I bet.

CATHERINE. I'm very happy.

GINNY. I always wanted to be a stewardess.

CATHERINE. Really?

GINNY. Uh-huh. (*An awkward pause.*) Are you absolutely positive I can't get you anything? Bobby?

BOBBY. C'mon, what are ya worried about, there'll be plenty of eats at the reunion.

GINNY. Are you sure? Really sure?

JERRY. I think maybe Catherine and Bobby would just like to sit down and rest for a few minutes. They had a long drive.

GINNY. Oh, of course! I'm not even letting you sit down. Sit down, sit down! (*She exits to bedroom to hang up coats. Catherine, Steve, and Bobby sit on couch. Catherine in the middle. An awkward pause.*)

CATHERINE. You all grew up together, is that right?

STEVE. Started grammar school together, and went right through to high school.

BOBBY. Yeah, then these guys went off to different colleges and left me in New Jersey to rot, ha ha. (*To Catherine.*) Did I ever tell ya I went to college?

CATHERINE. You did?

BOBBY. Sure. For about a month!

GINNY. (*She re-enters, lights a stick of incense.*) Oh! I didn't know that.

BOBBY. Didn't work out.

GINNY. I never went to college, either. Not that my grades weren't good enough. But at the time, my mother was all alone and I felt I had to make some kind of a decision, do you know what I mean?

CATHERINE. I only went to one of those two-year colleges myself. Before I became a stewardess.

GINNY. Did you like it?

CATHERINE. Oh, it was fun. I met lots of interesting people. (*During this section, Catherine opens her handbag, takes out the first jay of the evening, lights it and passes it around.*)

BOBBY. So, Stevie! What the hell's been happenin'?

GINNY. Steve is writing a TV program so that Jerry can star in it.

19

BOBBY. Hey, that's more like it! 'Bout time you guys started cookin'! Listen, ya got a part for *me* in this TV show?

STEVE. Certainly, I have you playing a nuclear physicist.

BOBBY. Certainly, certainly. That's your, no wait a minute, don't tell me, your whadayacallit type casting.

GINNY. Oh, Bobby, that's funny.

BOBBY. Yeah, I know. I got a sense a humor about myself.

GINNY. Well, you have the *right* attitude. It doesn't pay to take yourself too seriously, do you know what I mean? We loved your Christmas card last year.

BOBBY. Hey, didja? With the little Santa Claus stoned out of his head hallucinatin' up there at the North Pole? Ya liked that, huh?

GINNY. It was cute.

BOBBY. Yeah. I thought ya'd like it. Did Jerry like it? Jerry don't seem to be smilin' at nothin' here, that's why I'm askin'.

JERRY. I'm sorry. Jesus. Sure, I liked your card.

BOBBY. Hey, don't apologize.

JERRY. You'll just have to excuse me. I'm a little out of it.

GINNY. Jerry's just a little confused right now about his ultimate goals in life.

BOBBY. I can dig it.

JERRY. Ginny. Please.

BOBBY. Ya wanna talk about it, pal?

JERRY. No.

BOBBY. That's OK. I can dig it. I can appreciate where you're comin' from 'cause I have been there myself. Ya talk about goin' through some heavy changes!

GINNY. We were worried about you, Bobby. Until you called, we hadn't spoken to you in so long.

BOBBY. Yeah, it's been what? A year, year-and-a-half.

GINNY. We never knew where you were, if you were still playing or what. We thought you might have been in some kind of trouble, and we wanted to help.

BOBBY. Naw . . . I just got super-depressed is what it was. Playin' all those gigs in all those clubs. I never thought I'd get sick of the Jersey shore . . . I mean, that was my dream come true, if ya remember.

GINNY. I remember. Sure.

BOBBY. Yeah. It's a good life. Hell, it's a great life! But what the fuck does it mean? I started to worry about gettin' old. Stupid, right? But there I was. A real Gloomy Gus.

GINNY. That's so hard to believe.

BOBBY. Believe it. Believe it. Anyway, I got in with this group of real together people, and they talked with me and gave me some books to read and I guess ya could say brought me back to life . . . believe me, Jerry, I know where you're comin' from. Anytime ya need to have a serious talk about what's eatin' away your gut, makin' ya feel like ya gotta puke when ya get up in the mornin' . . . give me a call. Please. I'm serious.

JERRY. Thanks, Bobby.

BOBBY. 's all right, man.

GINNY. Are you playing any of your own material yet, Bobby?

BOBBY. Naw. Mostly, we do just the popular stuff—somethin' from Aerosmith, somethin' from Kiss, a little Zeppelin, the usual, y'know.

JERRY. Any Stones?

BOBBY. No way!

JERRY. You're kidding. You don't do anything by the Rolling Stones?

BOBBY. Kids don't wanna hear that shit. Sixties shit, that's what they call it. They think Mick Jagger's an old fart.

JERRY. Aw, no.

BOBBY. Yeah.

JERRY. What the hell's the matter with these kids today?! They think *Mick Jagger's* an old fart?

BOBBY. Better believe it. See, basically, in my job, ya can perform new shit, which is to say right now '70's shit, or ya can do '50's shit, mainly the ballad stuff for the slow numbers, but ya gotta stay away from '60's shit 'cause for some reason the kids just don't wanna hear it.

GINNY. That's fascinating.

BOBBY. Yeah, one night I figured the whole thing out. What it boils down to is cycles.

GINNY. How do you mean, Bobby?

BOBBY. C-Y-C-L-E-S. Cycles. Like ya have cycles of war and cycles of peace. And of course your washing machine has three basic cycles. It's the same with everything. People are born, people die, little people, called children, grow up and take their place. Ya follow what I'm talkin' about? I mean it's life, it's the way Jesus intended. And it's the same thing with music, man. So, the way I figure, '60's shit should become real, real popular again in the '80's, and '50's shit will probably be, like, modified, and become

21

the new music. Now, I really dig a lot of the sounds that were put down in the '60's, ya see what I'm sayin'? But what can I do? It's not my job to tell people what they should like, and besides, everything comes around again in the end, so it don't really matter. And I'll tell ya, I take great comfort from that, I mean I used to worry about gettin' old, but the beautiful thing, man, is that THERE IS NO SUCH THING! 'Cause somewhere out in space, or time . . . or someplace . . . all the moments of our lives are still goin' on . . . it's like this movie . . . and we're all in it . . . and after the universe is destroyed by, uh, whadaya-callit?

CATHERINE. Armageddon.

BOBBY. Right. After that happens, then everybody will realize that OUR ENTIRE PURPOSE on this fucking planet was just to sort of lay back, stay mellow, and go with the flow . . . and that's why, in this cosmic sense, it don't matter whether it's '50's shit or '60's shit or '70's shit or '40's shit or whatever . . . 'cause it's all the same shit!

STEVE. Bobby?

BOBBY. Yeah?

STEVE. May I tell you something?

BOBBY. Sure.

STEVE. In all honesty, I don't think you have the faintest idea of what you just said.

BOBBY. Guy's a pisser, ain't he? (*Laughing.*) You're somethin' else, man. Lemme tell ya. (*To Steve.*) You have not changed one bit in all the years I know ya. Ya just come right out and say what's on your mind . . . you're beautiful, man!

STEVE. What are you hugging me for?

BOBBY. 'Cause you're beautiful, man.

STEVE. I demand that you retract that statement immediately.

BOBBY. I love this man! Y'know, Steve, I tell ya— (*Steve and Bobby do an old routine from high school—slapping together hands, elbows, hips and so on in time with their words.*) a lotta people are gonna shit in their pants when you and me and Jerry walk in to that reunion— (*To Jerry.*) HEY!

GINNY. Jerry? (*Pause.*)

JERRY. I'm not going to the reunion, Bobby.

BOBBY. Not goin'? (*He indicates he thinks it's a joke—Steve mimics him.*)

JERRY. I'm just not up for it . . . and I would really appreciate it if I didn't have to discuss it. OK? (*There is a long pause.*)

BOBBY. That's a bummer. Well, shit, it's your own business, y'know. I mean . . . I was really lookin' forward to all of us goin' together. Do a little more smoke. Get really ripped, y'know? . . .

JERRY. I know. I'm sorry.

BOBBY. Freak out the folks back home . . .

JERRY. I'm sorry. Maybe, uh, the next reunion.

BOBBY. Hey, no problem. Ya don't have to apologize.

JERRY. Thanks, Bobby.

BOBBY. 's OK, man.

JERRY. Would anyone mind very much if I did some of my exercises?

BOBBY. What's there to mind?

CATHERINE. Of course not, Jerry.

JERRY. (*Spreading out blanket on floor.*) It's just very important that I do these exercises every day and I wasn't able to do them before, and I'm pretty high right now and if I wait around, I'll probably be too tired, so . . .

BOBBY. 's OK. (*Jerry starts to exercise. No one speaks. A kind of GLOOM settles over the room. With nothing to speak about, everyone gradually watches Jerry exercise.*)

STEVE. It's all right. He can't hear us now.

CATHERINE. I beg your pardon?

STEVE. He can't hear us now. He's exercising.

CATHERINE. You mean when he exercises . . .

STEVE. Exactly. Subconsciously, of course, he may be picking up a few stray words and phrases, but on the conscious level, he's no longer even aware of us. Just ignore him.

GINNY. Steve, don't make fun of Jerry!

STEVE. I wouldn't dream of making fun of Jerry. I know how important it is that he be allowed to work his aggressions out of his system in this relatively harmless manner. I know what the consequences would be if . . .

GINNY. Steve! What are you talking about?!

STEVE. I'm talking about the truth, Ginny. The ugly, painful truth that we've lived with for years. (*To Catherine.*) I've been with Jerry on days when he hasn't had time to exercise. He'd just start beating people up on the street.

CATHERINE. Oh no! Did he know these people? I mean—

STEVE. No. He'd just single someone out at random . . . an old man, a blind woman . . . and begin beating them up.

BOBBY. Violence, man, it's such a waste.

GINNY. Stephen!

STEVE. I'd try to hold him back, of course, but it was no use. Jerry, I'd say, he doesn't mean you any harm. Look, the poor man can barely walk, someday we'll be like that too. Please come home, Jerry. Give the man back his crutches. But it was no use, he wouldn't listen, he—

JERRY. (*Standing up.*) Hey, shut the fuck up!

GINNY. (*To Steve.*) Now you've upset him. Why do you make up those stories about Jerry?

CATHERINE. He was making all that up?

JERRY. YES! YES! And do you know why he was making that up? I'll tell you why he was making that up. Or would you rather tell them, Steve? Go ahead. Tell them why you were making up stories about me!

STEVE. Because I'm silly . . .

JERRY. That's right, Steve! Because you're silly! You're a silly man! And you know what, Steve? Now everybody in this room *knows* that you're a silly man. I know it. Bobby knows it. Ginny knows it. Catherine knows it. How does that make you feel, Steve?

STEVE. Silly . . .

JERRY. RIGHT! That's right. That's exactly how you should feel.

BOBBY. Aw, I knew Stevie was kiddin' around.

CATHERINE. Why didn't you tell *me?* (*To Ginny.*) Is Jerry really mad?

GINNY. (*To Steve.*) That *was* silly, Stephen.

STEVE. . . . I have no right to exist.

JERRY. I can help you solve that problem.

BOBBY. Hey, hey, hey! Let's put the conversation back on re-wind.

JERRY. I'm sorry, Bobby. I didn't mean to lose my temper in front of you and Catherine.

CATHERINE. It's perfectly all right.

GINNY. (*Hugging Jerry.*) Oh, Jerry, Jerry, Jerry, Jerry, Jerry, Jerry, Jerry!!

JERRY. What? What?

GINNY. (*Taking Jerry's hand.*) Come on and sit back down with me. Stephen, you will sit over there until you learn to behave.

STEVE. OK. (*Steve sits in upholstered chair* L. *While no one is watching, he casually picks up Jerry's discarded blanket and drapes it over his head.*)

GINNY. Jerry, I know what you're going through. I know how difficult . . .

STEVE. Is this all right?

24

GINNY. I don't think you're very funny, Stephen. (*To Jerry.*) I *know* how difficult everything seems. But it's times like these that we *need* other people. We shouldn't lock up our feelings inside us. We *need* people. *All* of us. Bobby, you know what I'm saying is true, don't you?

BOBBY. Hey, that's what it's all about, ain't it?

GINNY. OK—is everybody calm now? (*Back again to Jerry.*) I know how easy it seems to just want to give up . . .

JERRY. I don't want to give up. I just don't want to go to this reunion tonight.

GINNY. Jerry, you don't have to go to your reunion if you really don't want to . . . but—

JERRY. It's just that . . . there'll be a lot of people there that remember me . . . and they're all going to ask me the same question.

CATHERINE. What question, Jerry?

JERRY. "How's it going?"

GINNY. So?

JERRY. It's *not* going, it's *not* going, that's the point. My life is going nowhere. Look, you may not realize this, but certain people had extremely high hopes for me.

BOBBY. We still do, man.

JERRY. I wish you wouldn't say things like that, Bobby.

GINNY. Bobby didn't mean it.

BOBBY. I didn't mean it, Jerry.

JERRY. People didn't just think I'd do well in my profession. They had *extremely* high expectations for me. In fact, my guidance counsellor in high school—he was the one that really encouraged me to become an actor—he thought that . . . I had a gift . . . or something. His name was Doc Burns . . .

BOBBY. Doc Burns, hey, ya know I saw him a couple months ago out in Jersey. I was shopping around one of those Flea Markets down near Keansburg, ya know—

JERRY. Doc? You saw the Doc?

BOBBY. Oh yeah. He asked about ya.

JERRY. What did he say?

BOBBY. He said, "How's Jerry?"

JERRY. Hey, how *is* the Doc?

BOBBY. He was fired, ya know.

JERRY. Jesus, when?

BOBBY. Couple years ago, fired or laid off . . . I don't know.

25

JERRY. What's he doing?

BOBBY. Sellin' cosmetics. Had a cousin got him into the business. Got a little VW stuffed with all this shit. Travels around to the different Flea Markets. He said—

JERRY. But they can't fire Doc Burns! I mean, especially at his age—

BOBBY. No, he said he likes it.

JERRY. I know who was behind it. I bet it was that fucking asshole of a principal Conklin— (*Jerry rises and walks* D. *All but Catherine start to follow. Overlap.*)

BOBBY. Jerry, honest, he said he finally got used to it. Meets a lotta different people. Seemed like a really happy-go-lucky guy.

JERRY. —he always had it in for the Doc! That bastard! Boy, would I love to lay into that guy!

(*Ginny attempts to console Jerry.*)

BOBBY. (*To Steve.*) Maybe I shouldn't have brought up the subject. (*Steve attempts to console Bobby. During the following exchange, Catherine lights another jay, moves* D. *and offers Bobby the first hit.*)

GINNY. Jerry?

JERRY. I'm sorry, I just cannot accept this.

GINNY. Look, Jerry, I'm going to tell you something. You know where you're making a big mistake? You think you're the only person who's ever had these dreams. We've all had dreams and we've all had to give up certain dreams.

STEVE. Last night, I dreamed I was taking a shower with Catherine Deneuve. I had to give that up.

GINNY. Be quiet, Stephen. Jerry, have you ever taken the time to ask me what some of *my* dreams were? Did you know that in one way we have had very similar dreams?

JERRY. Ginny . . .

GINNY. Yes, Jerry, it's true, only *I* gave up my big dream a long, long time ago. At the age of 15, I came to the painful conclusion that I was not a genius! And I had always wanted to be a genius so badly. But alas, I could not do anything, I mean *anything!* I could not paint or dance, or write like Steve, or act like Jerry, or play music like Bobby, let alone, my goodness, be a genius! And and and and and—

JERRY. Take it easy. (*He tries to help her to the couch; she immediately sits down on the floor in front of it.*)

GINNY. —and I still had this desire to *understand* things, you know what I mean?

26

CATHERINE. Of course.

GINNY. Oh, I wanted to understand *everything*. The world that I lived in. The way people who could create *must* be able to understand the world they live in, and not be afraid of it, like when I was little—

JERRY. Ginny, please. (*She stops momentarily: embarrassed.*)

CATHERINE. Go on.

GINNY. . . . like, when I was little—I was always afraid of the dark, you know, boogie-boogie-boogie, so one night, my mother let me stay up, it was incredible, she came into my room where I was crying and we tiptoed downstairs, and the house was pitch dark except in the living room, and we ate crackers with jelly, and some chocolate milk . . .

JERRY. No one wants to hear this, Ginny.

STEVE. Are you kidding? This is great.

JERRY. Seriously. Is there anyone who really wants to hear this?

BOBBY. Graham crackers?

GINNY. Well, of course, silly, what else would you eat jelly and chocolate milk with?

BOBBY. What kinda jelly?

GINNY. Wait . . . strawberry!

BOBBY. Ya ever have apple butter? On graham crackers? Every afternoon, after school, we used to have ice-cold apple butter on graham crackers, I mean ya wanna taste somethin' unfuckingbelievable man—

GINNY. Wait a minute! What was I talking about? You made me forget! Oh, shit! What was I talking about? Now I can't remember! Oh, shit!

BOBBY. You were talkin' about apple butter.

CATHERINE. Bobby?

BOBBY. What?

CATHERINE. Bobby, *you* were talking about apple butter. Ginny was talking about being afraid of the dark when she was a little girl. Perhaps later this evening, we will have a discussion about apple butter. If that should happen, I think you should be the person to lead that discussion. *However,* until that moment—

BOBBY. Hey, Cee?

CATHERINE. Yes, Bobby?

BOBBY. Are you makin' fun of me?

CATHERINE. No, Bobby. I am not making fun of you.

BOBBY. I didn't think you were makin' fun of me.

CATHERINE. You were correct.

27

GINNY. Right! I've got it! So we had all this food and we had the TV on real quiet and we played a game of Old Maid and what happened was I was yawning and getting sleepy and all of a sudden, I noticed that there was something very, very bright shining through the curtains . . .

BOBBY. Wait! Don't tell me, it was the morning, right?

GINNY. Right! It was the sun! And my mother opened the curtains and she said: "Ta da!" (*Almost simultaneously, Steve and Bobby say "Ta da" to each other.*) Then she said, "Now Ginny I want you to go upstairs and get some sleep and from now on at night, if you get afraid of the dark, just remember how we sat up together and how nothing jumped out of the dark places to eat you." Then she said something I never forgot. She put me back to bed, and right before I fell asleep . . .

STEVE. (*Jumping up suddenly.*) Hear that?

GINNY. What?

STEVE. There's somebody out in the hall. (*He exits through door into hallway.*)

GINNY. Be careful. What am I saying? I didn't hear anybody.

CATHERINE. I'm positive I didn't hear anybody.

BOBBY. Hey, ya never can tell about these things!

CATHERINE. You're not getting paranoid, are you, honey? You shouldn't smoke so much if it's going to make you paranoid.

BOBBY. I'm fine . . . WHO THE FUCK IS IT, STEVE?!?!

CATHERINE. Bobby. Ssssh!

BOBBY. You hear that?

CATHERINE. Hear what, Bobby?

BOBBY. WHAT THE HELL'S GOIN' ON OUT THERE?? HEY, STEVIE!!

STEVE. (*Re-entering.*) He's gone.

BOBBY. Big guy?

GINNY. Steve, you're so full of shit, there wasn't anybody out there.

BOBBY. What he say?

STEVE. He said: Make sure . . .

BOBBY. Yeah?

STEVE. Make sure . . . you don't miss the reunion.

GINNY. Stephen, you're a real shit.

BOBBY. Hey, that's right. I did forget about the reunion.

CATHERINE. Well, *I* didn't forget about it. We have plenty of

28

time. Now I think we should let Ginny finish what she was trying to say before all this started.

GINNY. You know, Steve, you really piss me off.

STEVE. Yeah?

GINNY. I was honestly trying to express myself, and you weren't paying any attention to me. God knows expressing myself is something I rarely get to do around here with you and Jerry arguing all the time, and you weren't paying any fucking attention.

STEVE. Hey! You're serious.

GINNY. Well, I don't want to hurt your feelings, but . . .

CATHERINE. Say whatever you feel.

GINNY. But . . . it's like you think I wouldn't have anything very interesting to say, like you were somehow superior to whatever I might possibly be telling you.

STEVE. I didn't know you felt like that.

GINNY. You know what it's like? It's sort of like arrogance. Like you're really superior to other people. I don't know. Maybe it's not intentional . . .

STEVE. I really come across like that?

GINNY. Now, maybe it's just your way of coping with difficult situations, in which case it's cool and I can understand it, but you should be aware that other people do notice.

STEVE. Really?

GINNY. Well, I would say they do, I mean, because *I* notice it. Anyway, where was I? (*Catherine has lit another joint and passes it to Ginny.*) Hmmmmn. Thank you. Hmmmmn, this is good, thank you. So, anyway, the point of the story—where was I?

STEVE. (*To Ginny—quietly.*) Your mother put you back to bed.

GINNY. Oh, right! (*She pauses, looks at Steve.*) Thank you. (*Back to the group.*) So. OK, here we go, I got it, so, my mother put me back to bed, and just before I fell asleep, she said: "Remember, Ginny, the dark is just a *great big warm room* with all the lights out. Just 'cause you can't see the room sometimes doesn't mean it isn't there." Uh, THE END.

BOBBY. Sure . . . and that's like when ya die is when Jesus turns on the lights for ya and then ya can laugh at what scared ya all your life, right? (*Everyone slowly turns and stares at Bobby.*)

BOBBY. What?

GINNY. All of a sudden. I just had this terrific rush.

JERRY. Are my legs still on?

29

CATHERINE. Oh, so did I.

STEVE. I cannot move.

BOBBY. Good shit, huh, Stevie?

CATHERINE. It's so peaceful . . . just sitting around . . . talking. Do you do this often?

GINNY. Well . . . we . . .

CATHERINE. We're always out. Bobby's usually playing. Or we're going to watch somebody else playing. Or I'm flying . . . (*Jerry imagines Catherine literally flying and goes into a stoned laughing fit—the others "get it" one by one and start laughing also—even Catherine.*) What I mean is: what do you do for fun?

JERRY. This is it.

GINNY. Jerry—

STEVE. Now that Jerry's entering the sunset years we feel it best to avoid overexcitement.

CATHERINE. You don't travel? You don't go to concerts or movies?

GINNY. Well, of course, not every night, but—

JERRY. This is it.

STEVE. It's very simple. Jerry told Ginny he won't take her to see a movie until he gets a part in one.

GINNY. Stephen . . .

STEVE. Which is certainly a fair request, don't you think?

GINNY. (*To Catherine.*) It's not true.

JERRY. (*To* STEVE.) Hey . . .

STEVE. What?

CATHERINE. (*To Ginny.*) So do you watch a lot of television?

GINNY. It's broken. We're going to have it fixed.

CATHERINE. There's a special on tonight . . . on the Golden Age of Television.

GINNY. And we're missing it, oh I'm sorry. I guess I'm not a very good hostess.

CATHERINE. Don't be silly. It's on much later, and we couldn't watch it anyway.

GINNY. Who are they showing?

CATHERINE. Oh God—everybody. George Burns and Gracie Allen. Sid Caesar and Imogene Coca. Milton Berle. Captain Video—

BOBBY. —and his Video Rangers. Used to love those guys. (*To Jerry.*) You still got your helmet?

JERRY. My what?

30

BOBBY. Your helmet. Your space helmet.

JERRY. No, I do not still have my space helmet. Do you still have *your* space helmet?

BOBBY. Naw. What am I gonna do with a space helmet? I was just kiddin'.

JERRY. I know.

BOBBY. They were fun, though.

JERRY. They were.

STEVE. (*To Bobby.*) You violated a solemn oath.

BOBBY. I did?

STEVE. All honorary video rangers swore they would never throw out their official helmets. You realize I'm going to have to report you for this?

BOBBY. Don't report me!

CATHERINE. —Dave Garroway, and Red Skelton, and Edward R. Murrow, and Jack Benny, and . . .

GINNY. . . . I used to have such a crush on Edward R. Murrow.

CATHERINE. Really? I never had a television romance until JFK. When he looked into the camera and told the nation that there were missiles in Cuba, he was incredibly sexy, I thought.

GINNY. Edward R. Murrow may not have been sexy, but he looked just like my father. And they both died from too many cigarettes.

CATHERINE. Oh, I'm sorry.

GINNY. My father was beautiful. He always wore these very clean white shirts. He'd come home from the factory and take a shower and then put on one of his clean white shirts. He used to smoke Camel cigarettes which were very clean and white because nobody smoked filters then on account of nobody knew what cigarettes could do to you and he used to read the evening paper and smoke. I used to just sit sometimes, in the corner of the couch, pretending to be taking a nap, and watch my father, in his clean white shirt, his hair all wet and combed back and shining, smoking his little white cigarettes. He was beautiful. (*Pause.*)

BOBBY. Could I have a glass of soda?

GINNY. Sure, Bobby.

BOBBY. Thanks. (*No one moves. It should be clear that they're all very stoned.*)

CATHERINE. I was in high school during the Cuban missile crisis. When the blockade went into effect, they led us downstairs into the basement, and the nuns stood around and everyone had

31

to say the rosary because people really believed that a nuclear war could have broken out that morning. I didn't want to stay there. I didn't want to die like that. I was near a flight of steps that led upstairs and when no one was looking, I snuck out. I just . . . wanted to be outside. I had never been disobedient or questioned authority before that moment.

BOBBY. (*Appreciatively.*) All right . . . !

CATHERINE. It was cold outside and there was an incredible blue sky and no wind. There were no people. I walked around the empty schoolyard. I was so afraid. There were tears in my eyes because I really believed I was looking at everything for the last time. It was so beautiful. I felt like a little girl. I began to touch things. The brick wall of the school. The iron railing of the fence that ran around the yard. The bicycle rack. Everything was so cold and yet so beautiful. I filled my lungs with air. I was alive. I had never admitted to myself how much I loved just being alive. And I knew if I survived, I would never forget that morning when I had wanted to touch and feel everything around me. I was sixteen at this time. A virgin . . . After the crisis had passed, I still felt like I was moving through a very beautiful dream. I had a date with Greg Sutton, the captain of the basketball team, very soon after. That night, without even realizing that I was saying the words, I begged Greg to fuck me. He couldn't believe it. He was probably a virgin, too. I said, Greg, all of us are on this earth for only a short while, and we can't be afraid, we have to open ourselves up to every moment . . . so Greg fucked me in the back seat of his car that cold winter's night at the drive-in. Moonlight shone through the windows. I can't begin to describe what it was like. I can only ask you to imagine it. In and out. In and out. In and out. I wrapped my legs around him and I remembered how beautiful and precious the world had seemed to me that morning and I grabbed at him repeatedly and plunged my tongue deep inside his mouth. My breasts were heaving up and down. I was so hot and wet. It was indescribable . . . I can only ask you to try and imagine this. Anyway, after that night, Greg must have done some bragging to his friends, because the next week I was literally besieged with requests for dates. All of which I accepted. Greg became jealous, but I explained to him that I needed to reach out and touch everyone for myself, just as, that morning, I had wanted to touch every leaf on the big oak tree outside the school when I thought the world would perish in a fiery holocaust. Be-

32

fore the term was over, I had gone to bed with over twenty different boys. And my geometry teacher, Mr. Handfield. That summer, I took a house with some girls down at the Jersey shore. College boys were in and out of that house every night, and I denied myself nothing. At long last, I became a stewardess and travelled all over the world and had innumerable sexual experiences with men of every race and culture imaginable . . . also, I was able to see the clouds close up, which I had always wanted to do. I wanted to reach out and touch them. I still do. Perhaps some day I will . . . But I have never lost the joy of just being alive ever since that morning in 1962. Bobby always tells me I'm the most passionate person he knows, in or out of bed, and he understands why, although I love him, I have to have the freedom to reach out and touch and commune with my fellow human creatures. Because we are all on this earth for only a very short while . . . And I just can't get depressed by that . . . (*Pause.*)

BOBBY. Could I have a glass of soda?

GINNY. Of course, Bobby.

BOBBY. Thanks. (*But no one moves—still very stoned.*)

GINNY. What is—?

CATHERINE. Yes? Please go on.

GINNY. What is your ultimate goal in life, Catherine?

CATHERINE. My ultimate goal in life is to live on the moon.

BOBBY. Hey, this is news to me . . .

CATHERINE. I don't think the subject ever came up before, Bobby.

BOBBY. . . . the moon!?

CATHERINE. Yes.

BOBBY. Well, I guess ya know that's gonna pull the plug on our livin' together.

CATHERINE. It won't even be possible for many years yet, Bobby.

BOBBY. Good.

STEVE. You should never have thrown away your helmet!

GINNY. It *will* be possible, though, won't it? I mean, not right away, but in our lifetime. People will be living . . . OUT THERE!

CATHERINE. (*With a certain amount of pride.*) Yes.

GINNY. Brrr. It's scary.

CATHERINE. Oh, well I think it's just so exciting! I mean, everything is changing! Our whole world is changing, and nobody

33

knows what's going to happen next, and here we all are, at this extraordinary moment in time, and we're alive and, really, what could be more exciting than that?

STEVE. Ralph Kramden coming home from work and finding Alice in bed with Ed Norton.

BOBBY. Holy shit!

STEVE. Now that's what I call exciting!

GINNY. That's sick.

STEVE. Now let's see: he'd be completely naked except for his sewer workers' gloves and his hat, and . . .

JERRY. Excuse me, Steve. (*To Catherine.*) You know what I think is really exciting? That there'll be a record of all of it—how we lived—because we have movies and television and people in the future will be able to see us and—

CATHERINE. Oh, I just think it's fascinating!

JERRY. You really think so?

CATHERINE. Well, I just think it's a wonderful thing that we can preserve these images of ourselves for the future.

JERRY. Yeah. And the same goes for all the people at Woodstock, right? I mean, because of the movie. The moment was saved.

CATHERINE. That's a very good example.

JERRY. You know, I had a chance to go up there with all these kids, but I turned it down. I thought it was all some kind of publicity stunt. I was staying with my uncle and working in his factory that summer, and I guess it was about 7:30 in the morning, real hot, I was walking to work, feeling pretty good, and I stopped to watch this caravan of cars go past me, all these bedrolls tied on top, with banners that said "Woodstock or Bust," and all these kids waved at me and I waved at them, we were laughing, they wanted me to come with them. I was laughing because I thought they were crazy. It was literally a fucking caravan. Then I couldn't see them because of the dust, and when it cleared they were gone. There wasn't anybody else around—I just stood there, holding my thermos, looking down the road after them, wondering if . . . you know. Then I turned around and walked down this path to the factory, and all through the morning and into the afternoon, while I was driving around in this fork-lift, stacking palettes, this caravan of cars was making its way to Woodstock, and into the history books. And I missed it. (*Bobby and Steve, through looks and gestures, console Jerry. Their concern for him makes him*

34

self-conscious.) Hey, what am I saying? The important thing is where are we now? What are we feeling now? I mean *all* of us.

BOBBY. Right!

JERRY. Woodstock, Jesus! Talk about not being able to confront your past. I've been making myself sick all these years thinking there was something there I missed, and it was probably nothing more than a lot of muddy sleeping bags and bad acid trips.

BOBBY. Yeah.

JERRY. I mean: who the hell knows? (*To Catherine.*) Were you at Woodstock?

CATHERINE. (*She has gone into a reverie during Jerry's story.*) *Yes I was . . .*

JERRY. How was it?

CATHERINE. It was *beautiful*. One of the most beautiful memories I'll ever have in my life. You would have loved it, Jerry.

JERRY. Thank you.

GINNY. Let me see you smile. Come on, you were smiling just before. Don't stop now.

JERRY. *Ginny. Please.*

CATHERINE. I'm *so* sorry, I certainly didn't mean—

GINNY. (*To Catherine.*) Don't worry about it.

BOBBY. (*To Catherine.*) Hey! Ya know?

CATHERINE. I'm *so* sorry.

GINNY. (*Laughing.*) Catherine, for goodness' sake, don't apologize. (*To Jerry.*) Let me see you smile—all those who want to see Jerry smile raise their hands. (*Everyone raises hands.*) It's unanimous! Now you have to smile. Hey Bobby, would you do me a favor?

BOBBY. Name it.

GINNY. Would you take off Jerry's socks and tickle his feet?

BOBBY. My pleasure.

JERRY. Bobby, please.

GINNY. And while you do that, I'm going to go to work on his stomach.

CATHERINE. Can I do anything?

GINNY. I don't think so, Catherine. Bobby and I should be able to handle this.

STEVE. He's starting to smile.

JERRY. I am not starting to smile. Now can we please begin behaving like adults? Or are some of us still children? (*Pause.*)

35

BOBBY. Shit. Maybe Jerry's right.

GINNY. What do you think, Bobby?

BOBBY. I dunno. What do you think, Ginny? (*They smile at each other and tickle Jerry.*)

JERRY. Cut it out! C'mon, stop it! Hey! Hey!

GINNY. Kootchie! Kootchie! Kootchie!

JERRY. OK, everybody! C'mon! Stop it! Stop! Hey!

GINNY. Smile, godammit!

JERRY. No!

BOBBY. Laugh, you ugly mother, laugh! (*Jerry laughs as they continue to tickle him; Steve gets Poloroid and snaps Jerry's picture; Jerry crawls away from them.*)

GINNY. We did it! We did it!

JERRY. That wasn't fair.

GINNY. Be quiet. You loved it.

JERRY. I did not love it. And I'm still not going to the reunion, so—

GINNY. Sssssssh!

JERRY. —if that's what you're thinking, you can—

GINNY. (*She covers his mouth with her hand.*) Sssssssh! (*She removes her hand.*)

JERRY. Don't do that! (*He pulls away from her.*)

GINNY. (*She hugs him.*) Sssssssh . . . I love you. (*She kisses him on the forehead.*) That's for looking so cute when you were laughing.

JERRY. Why do you always want me to be laughing? Why don't you listen to me when I try to talk to you?

GINNY. Jerry, when was the last time you really *tried* to talk to me?

JERRY. I don't want you to do things just because of me.

GINNY. You mean: not anymore you don't.

JERRY. What's that supposed to mean?

STEVE. Hey.

CATHERINE. Jerry, I want to apologize if what I said before—

JERRY. Apologize? Oh come on, what is this, I feel bad enough about ruining this evening for everybody, please don't—

BOBBY. Ya didn't ruin no evening! Come on, will ya? I hate to see ya talk like that.

JERRY. I'm the one who should be apologizing—

GINNY. I love you . . . (*She embraces Jerry.*)

BOBBY. I love *you*, beautiful lady.

36

CATHERINE. I love *you*, Bobby. (*They kiss.*)

GINNY. And who do *you* love, Stephen?

STEVE. Catherine Deneuve. I write her letters, care of Chanel No. 5. She never answers them. Each morning I walk to my mail slot, close my eyes—press my nose against the metal grill and sniff. Nothing. Some mornings it's even worse, I can't sleep, I get up and roam the streets, searching for my mailman . . .

JERRY. Does anyone know what time it is?

BOBBY. What is time? Ya know what I mean? What is time? (*Bobby and Catherine resume kissing.*)

GINNY. (*To the rescue.*) I'm going to have some soda. Would anybody like some soda? Catherine?

CATHERINE. (*Coming out of kiss.*) All right.

GINNY. Steve?

STEVE. I'll have whatever Jerry's having.

GINNY. Jerry?

JERRY. Nothing.

STEVE. (*To Ginny.*) Put a little whipped cream on mine, would you?

GINNY. I'll take care of you Stephen. Bobby?

BOBBY. Sure . . . I'll have another glass of soda. (*Ginny exits to kitchen. Another uneasy silence. Catherine tries to break the ice.*)

CATHERINE. How long have you and Ginny been living here?

JERRY. Long.

CATHERINE. I noticed you have a bathtub in the kitchen.

JERRY. Yes.

CATHERINE. I noticed it when we came in.

JERRY. Everyone notices it.

CATHERINE. I've never seen a bathtub in a kitchen.

JERRY. We insisted on it.

STEVE. In the winter, when the landlord shuts off the heat, Jerry converts the bathtub into a skating rink for the mice. Yes, many's the time I've found Jerry leaning over the tub with a big grin on his face, watching the little guys whizzing and slipping all over, their mufflers crackling in the breeze, jumping over rows of tiny barrels.

BOBBY. Stevie's just like I told ya, ain't he?

CATHERINE. Exactly!

STEVE. Jerry, that was a joke! You know, when you're a big star in my comedy series which you still don't believe is going to hap-

37

pen, you're going to say to me: "Steve, thank you. Thank you for teaching me to laugh at myself. Thank you for bringing a little sunshine into my life."

JERRY. Steve, seriously, what if the script doesn't sell?

STEVE. Are you kidding? It can't miss. Norman Lear will love this script.

JERRY. Just assume that you might not be able to sell this script, Steve. OK? Will you be content to spend the rest of your life getting stoned and watching re-runs of Abbott and Costello every morning before you leave for work? Then walking around—

STEVE. Are you finished?

JERRY. Walking around the bookstore with a notebook under your arm, telling college girls that you're a famous writer?

STEVE. I never told them I was famous.

GINNY. (*Re-entering with the drinks.*) Ta da!

BOBBY and STEVE. Ta da!

JERRY. What if the script *doesn't* sell, Steve? When you got out of college, you wrote poetry for three years. Did you ever sell any poetry?

STEVE. When you got out of college, you wanted to give expression to the hopes and fears of our generation—your own words, and I quote from memory. Do you feel you've accomplished this as an actor?

JERRY. Did you ever sell any poetry?

STEVE. Nobody sells poetry, you just get it printed up in those little magazines. Jesus.

JERRY. Did you ever sell any poetry?

STEVE. No, I never sold any poetry, did you become the Marlon Brando of our generation? Do you now own a chain of islands in Tahiti? Are they selling posters with your picture on them in Times Square?

JERRY. Then you started writing short stories—did you ever—

STEVE. No, I never sold a short story. So what? What do you tell casting directors when they ask you about *your* accomplishments? "Well, for a couple of years, I, uh, was sort of hoping to give expression to the hopes and fears of my generation, and although about 1500 people have told me that I'm not right for the part, blah blah blah . . ."

JERRY. And then came the novel.

BOBBY. Hey, don't you guys want any a this soda?

JERRY. The novel which was turned down by how many publishers?

STEVE. (*To the group.*) I don't know about any of you, but I really love this.

JERRY. The novel which was turned down by how many publishers? Thirty?

STEVE. Thirty-one! And what do you mean: what do I tell all the girls who come in the bookstore? What do you tell all the girls who work in the office with *you*? And what do you tell your boss? Has anybody ever met Jerry's boss? (*Doing an impression of Jerry's boss.*) Beautiful man. "Jerry, vhen you are through playin' Hamlett und all dose udder crasy guys, you tink you vant to maybe stable togedder a couple of pages und empty da vastebasket, pleaze??"

JERRY. Steve. What if the script doesn't sell?

STEVE. Christ! I'll bet you that within six months to a year, I won't even need to be working in the fucking bookstore, and you'll be able to quit your office job for good. What do you say to that?

GINNY. *I* believe you, Stephen.

STEVE. Thank you.

JERRY. I'd say you're too late. (*Pause.*) I was fired last week.

STEVE. Wait a minute. Are you kidding?

JERRY. I've just been pretending to go to work every morning.

GINNY. You lost your job? My God, why didn't you tell me?

BOBBY. Oh, shit. More problems.

JERRY. I really didn't mean to lay this on everybody—

CATHERINE. I didn't even know you had a job—

JERRY. It was just a part-time job—a survival job—it wasn't important—

BOBBY. Jerry, I'm sorry ya lost your job.

GINNY. You didn't tell me.

BOBBY. I know what a bummer that is.

JERRY. Look, I shouldn't have mentioned this, I'm sorry, it's not important—

CATHERINE. But if it wasn't important, why mention it at all?

JERRY. Huh?

CATHERINE. (*To Ginny.*) He must have wanted to talk about it, or he wouldn't have told us.

JERRY. What?

STEVE. Thanks a lot for confiding in me, by the way.

CATHERINE. (*To Jerry.*) Am I right?

GINNY. I just can't believe you didn't feel you could tell me.

JERRY. (*To Ginny.*) It's not that I didn't *want* to tell you—

STEVE. (*Cutting him off.*) Then why didn't you?

JERRY. Because there was more to it than just getting fired, and if I thought I could make you understand that—

STEVE. Sure!

JERRY. Look. Manager calls me into his office and says: "We've been doing some thinking and we've decided to let you go." Just like that.

CATHERINE. Did he give you a reason?

JERRY. He said I'd been taking off too often to go to auditions.

CATHERINE. Did you want to get fired?

BOBBY. Hey, what are you doin'?

JERRY. One minute I know where I am, next minute I'm taking the elevator downstairs—I'm outside on the street, the sun is shining, and I don't know what to do—

CATHERINE. Did you *want* to get fired? (*An uneasy silence. Catherine submits her diagnosis.*) This is very clear to me.

BOBBY. She thinks she's a doctor.

JERRY. What do you mean?

CATHERINE. Well, it's like people feel the first time they're going to take a trip by plane. Last week, this man was boarding our flight, and right before the final step at the top of the ramp, he just stopped. I said—is this your first time? It took him five minutes before he even heard me talking to him, then he claimed he didn't know where he was or how he'd gotten there or which way to go, and I said—well, look, you've got a ticket in your hand, you must've known what you were doing, everybody's a little afraid the first time, if you don't come aboard *right now* we're going to have to leave without you.

JERRY. And he came aboard?

CATHERINE. No . . . he turned around, ran back down the ramp, across the field, and as far as I could see, he was still running when he reached the terminal.

JERRY. Yeah. I know, I felt afraid, too.

CATHERINE. Of course you did. Because you knew you would have to begin all over again, there was nothing holding you, you were free to change, but how could you be expected to know into what?

BOBBY. Ginny, what's the matter?

40

GINNY. Nothing.

BOBBY. C'mon, don't let none of this shit bother ya, everything's gonna work out OK.

GINNY. I'm very confused.

BOBBY. Too much smoke?

GINNY. Maybe . . . how can you smoke so much and still drive?

BOBBY. Years of practice.

GINNY. You *are* sure you can still drive?

BOBBY. Can Fred Astaire still dance?

GINNY. I mean . . . I want you all to arrive safely at the reunion.

BOBBY. Don't tell me *you're* not goin' now?

JERRY. Ginny, I don't understand why you *don't* want to go to the reunion with Steve.

GINNY. You don't?

STEVE. She doesn't have to go with me if she doesn't want to.

GINNY. I didn't say I didn't want to, Stephen!

STEVE. Because if she doesn't want to go with me, I'd just as soon stay home and finish that crossword puzzle in TV Guide—

BOBBY. Hey, what is this? What the hell is goin' on here? I don't know what's the matter with everybody anymore! *I don't see what the problem is:* we were sposed to go to this reunion, so let's go to this reunion! I don't wanna hear no more about anybody else not goin'! You're all gonna have a good time! First Jerry says he ain't goin' which I try to understand—

JERRY. Hey, Bobby!

BOBBY. Then *she* says she's not sure about goin', then *he* says if she don't go, *he* don't go— (*Bobby breaks down in tears.*)

STEVE. Bobby, I was only kidding!

CATHERINE. Bobby, don't cry. (*To Ginny.*) Just leave him alone. He'll be fine.

GINNY. Oh no, I was afraid this would happen. I didn't mean to upset you. (*To Steve.*) Can't you do something?

STEVE. Do what?

GINNY. I don't know. *Do something.*

STEVE. What am I going to do?

GINNY. Anything!

STEVE. Bobby. Watch me. (*He puts on gorilla mask. During his act, Bobby cheers up and starts laughing.*) Impression of Jerry watching a Laurel & Hardy movie. (*He slumps in his seat, arms crossed in angry fashion in front of him, watching the "movie."*) Impression of Jerry

41

watching a Marx Brothers movie. (*He slumps lower in his seat, tilting his head to one side.*)

GINNY. Actually, we rarely get to the movies. I mean, *I* rarely get to the . . .

STEVE. Impression of Jerry watching a W. C. Fields movie. (*Now he crosses his legs as well as his arms, turns chair to one side, looking gloomily at the screen over his shoulder.*)

BOBBY. (*Happy again.*) Hey Stevie, ya know who ya remind me of wearin' that mask?

STEVE. Your brother, Nicky?

BOBBY. Hey!

STEVE. I'm sorry.

BOBBY. Ya know my brother Nicky can't help the way he looks!

STEVE. (*Somewhat ashamed.*) I'm sorry. I don't know why I said that.

CATHERINE. Bobby, who *does* Stevie remind you of?

BOBBY. *You* know. Every time they show it, we get really stoned and sit in the first row?

CATHERINE. *2001.*

BOBBY. Yeah.

CATHERINE. (*She sees the screen in front of her.*) "The Dawn of Man."

BOBBY. Right. The part with all the gorillas.

GINNY. I never saw that movie.

CATHERINE. You never saw *2001?*

GINNY. I don't keep up with movies. But if it's really that good. (*Steve, still wearing mask, will act out everything Catherine says, pretending Ginny is his "mate."*)

CATHERINE. There's this absolutely incredible opening where we see our ancestors, who are, of course, these gross apes, on the verge of becoming men. We see them learning to use weapons to kill their prey with . . . and then we see them alone at night . . . it's very beautiful . . . looking out at the stars . . . which they do not understand . . . and they huddle together in their simple caves in order to keep each other warm . . . protected from the elements . . . from the wind and the rain . . . and their eyes are bright with fear and wonder as they prepare to become men and confront the mystery of the universe. (*Pause.*)

BOBBY. Those were the days, all right.

CATHERINE. (*Mystified.*) What days, Bobby?

BOBBY. When the *picture* came out—

CATHERINE. Oh! (*She starts to laugh.*)

STEVE. (*Taking off mask.*) Holy shit!

GINNY. What?

STEVE. There was this crazy girl I went to see *2001* with. She was one of those girls—

GINNY. —*Women*. Girls are children—women are not children.

STEVE. Right—this crazy woman I went out with for about a year.

CATHERINE. What was this crazy woman's name?

STEVE. This crazy woman's name was Laura.

GINNY. What did she look like?

STEVE. Remember, Jerry, I wrote you a letter and said I met this girl, Laura?

JERRY. I remember the letter. You remember writing me that you had fallen in love and were going to ask her to marry you?

CATHERINE. Ah ha!

GINNY. Stephen?

BOBBY. Kowabunga!

STEVE. Right, right—it was a pure Hollywood ending. I mean, our last day together. The final scene. In the rain, no less. And her telling me with tears in her eyes that I was living in this fantasy world. Right? Now, you have to picture this: the rain, the two of us standing together on the sidewalk, not moving, just looking at each other, in close-up, the camera cutting back and forth between our faces. This warm Spring rain . . .

GINNY. (*Shutting her eyes.*) Yes, I can see it!

STEVE. (*He's having fun, still in control, the Movie Director—but as he continues, it is clear that the memory controls him.*) And then she said goodbye, and turned, and walked away. And as I watched her, I could feel the camera pulling back for a long shot . . .

GINNY. (*With eyes still closed.*) I can see it.

STEVE. . . . and I felt her about to become a memory and I remembered watching her walking with her friends, it was like a slow-motion flashback you know, in the rain, or singing, the wind blowing her hair . . . and I ran after her and I held her shoulders and . . . I turned her around and I said to her: the very first time I saw you, you were walking in the rain, I saw you from a window in the library, and you were soaked and you looked so helpless, the leaves were all over you, and even though I didn't know who you were, I wanted to take off my coat and put it around you, which you would never have let me do, but I thought

43

at that moment . . . that it would have been possible not to be afraid of anything . . . if only I could place my coat around someone I loved . . . and pretend that I could protect her . . . I just wanted to tell you that . . .

GINNY. (*With her eyes still closed, in a dream.*) . . . Thank you.

STEVE. (*After a moment.*) What? . . .

GINNY. (*Opening her eyes.*) . . . Did you say something?

STEVE. . . . Did *you* say something?

GINNY. . . . I don't think so . . .

CATHERINE. . . . Ginny, you will be going to the reunion with us, won't you? There's *so* much I'd like to talk to you about.

GINNY. What?

CATHERINE. You are coming to the reunion . . . aren't you?

STEVE. (*Still somewhat in a trance.*) I just wanted to tell you that.

GINNY. I don't know . . . I don't know what to do . . .

CATHERINE. Oh, don't let it worry you, *nobody* knows what to do.

GINNY. They don't?

CATHERINE. Of course not. It's just like this very brilliant psychologist, whose name escapes me at the moment, but whom I usually have dinner with whenever I'm on stopover in Paris, is writing a book about "Contemporary Manifestations of"—something-or-other—anyway, I would say . . . uh . . . well, first, of course, I would address him by his name—I would say: "You know, uh, Jean, or Claude, or Francois, or whatever, there are times when I just become terribly confused about everything, and I don't know what to do"—and then he'd bring out this manuscript of his, Contemporary Manifestations of—

BOBBY. Boy, am I ever sick of hearin' about this fucking doctor!

CATHERINE. Robert!

BOBBY. Hey! She wants to ball this egghead—fine! No problem! I can dig that part of it. I'm a mature person. What I mean is when *we're* at home in the sack, she starts throwin' all of these ten-dollar words at me. But I mean I'm very patient with her, I tell her: Hey, give me a fuckin' break, you're givin' me a headache, for Chrissake! See my point? I mean, Jerry, did *you* know what she was talkin' about to you before? In all honesty, now?

JERRY. Well . . . yeah. I mean—

BOBBY. Ya did?

JERRY. I did, yeah.

BOBBY. Ginny?

44

GINNY. Well . . .

BOBBY. Well what?

GINNY. Well . . . a little, sort of . . .

BOBBY. See, well, I guess that's cause you're smarter than me.

GINNY. Bobby, that's not true!

JERRY. Hey Bobby, come on!

BOBBY. Who am I kiddin'? Abbott and Costello were probably smarter than me! Ralph fucking Kramden was probably smarter than me! The three fucking Stooges were—

CATHERINE. Robert! (*Pause. Bobby slowly realizes what he's been saying.*) Are you through?

BOBBY. Hey, Cee, Jesus, I just got carried away. Ya know how I get sometimes.

CATHERINE. Are you through?

BOBBY. I'm fine, I'm fine, just go ahead with what—

CATHERINE. That was negative energy, Bobby.

BOBBY. I hear what you're sayin'. (*He notices Steve in trance.*) What's the matter with Stevie? (*To Ginny.*) Is somethin' the matter with Stevie?

GINNY. Oh no! I hate when this happens.

JERRY. Hey, Steve!

CATHERINE. What is it?

JERRY. Hey, Steve!

BOBBY. What's the matter with Stevie?

GINNY. It's been so long since this happened. Stephen?

CATHERINE. This is fascinating.

GINNY. What you have to understand is that Stephen isn't like other people.

CATHERINE. Yes, I can see that.

GINNY. I mean he's extremely sensitive—I mean—

CATHERINE. Will he be all right?

GINNY. Yes. He just won't remember what he said.

CATHERINE. (*To Jerry.*) Does this happen often?

JERRY. Only when Steve is forced to deal with reality. About once or twice a year.

GINNY. Well, at least he's trying. Certain things take time, you know.

JERRY. I know.

BOBBY. (*Beginning to shiver.*) Hey Stevie, get a g-g-grip on yourself.

CATHERINE. Bobby?

45

BOBBY. I'll b-b-b-b-be O-ka-ka-ka-kay!

CATHERINE. Yes, Bobby. I *know* you'll be OK. The question is: when?

BOBBY. S-s-s-s-s-s-soon.

GINNY. My God!

CATHERINE. It's nothing . . . (*To Bobby.*) I love you, Bobby.

BOBBY. And I lu-lu-lu-lu-lu-love ya-ya-ya-ya-ya-ya—

GINNY. Catherine, isn't there anything I can do?

CATHERINE. Do you have any cake?

GINNY. Cake?

CATHERINE. Actually, anything very sweet and soft and gooey . . . ?

BOBBY. Twee-twee—

CATHERINE. What?

BOBBY. Twee-twee—

GINNY. Oh, my God! What's the matter with him?

CATHERINE. Bobby?

BOBBY. —twee-twee—

GINNY. He thinks he's some kind of bird!

BOBBY. Twee-twee-Twinkees!

GINNY. Twinkees? Gee, I'm not sure. Let me check. (*Ginny exits to kitchen as Catherine nurses Bobby.*)

STEVE. (*Coming out of trance.*) Naturally, it took me a month or two to get over her breaking up with me.

CATHERINE. Steve?

STEVE. But that's normal . . . (*He has just heard Catherine's voice.*) Did you say something?

CATHERINE. Steve, are you all right?

STEVE. Of course, I'm all right. Hey, what's the matter with Bobby?

CATHERINE. He just got a little nervous. He'll be fine. Bobby, look who's here. It's Steve.

BOBBY. Twee-twee—

CATHERINE. They're coming, Bobby.

GINNY. (*Enters with box of Devil Dogs.*) Will Devil Dogs do?

CATHERINE. Will Devil Dogs do? I don't know. Let's ask Bobby. Look Bobby, Dev—

BOBBY. (*Grabbing the box before she finishes.*) Th-th-th-thank God!

CATHERINE. (*As they all watch him eat.*) He'll be fine now.

STEVE. Devil Dogs?

GINNY. Stephen, you're back with us again! How do you feel?

46

(*Both Ginny and Catherine sit back down and sip their drinks. It should be clear that they are beginning to feel tired.*)

STEVE. I feel great!

GINNY. Are you sure?

STEVE. Yes! . . . Please don't look at me like that.

GINNY. If you don't feel all right, you shouldn't be afraid to say something.

STEVE. I feel fine. A little sleepy.

BOBBY. We gotta pull ourselves together, Stevie.

STEVE. What?

BOBBY. Well, you mainly. Ya keep flippin' out.

STEVE. Yeah, sure.

BOBBY. Ya want a Devil Dog, Stevie? I don't think I can eat all these.

CATHERINE. Well, I don't think anyone expects you to eat all 24 of them.

STEVE. Give me one.

BOBBY. Straighten ya right out.

STEVE. Straighten *me* right out?

BOBBY. Jerry, ya want a Devil Dog? Anybody else want a Devil Dog?

GINNY. I'm on a diet.

BOBBY. In that case, ya only get two. (*He throws two to her.*) Hey Jerry, ya want a Devil Dog? (*Jerry shakes his head.*)

STEVE. Straighten *me* right out? (*He laughs.*)

BOBBY. Just relax, Stevie. You'll be OK.

STEVE. (*To Ginny.*) Do you hear what he's saying? Isn't that incredible?

GINNY. (*Busy eating—hasn't heard a word he's said.*) Hmmmmmn?

STEVE. I said if you're on a diet, why do you keep a box of these in the kitchen? (*Ginny, still busy eating, points an accusing finger at Jerry.*) Oh. You only keep them here for Jerry?

GINNY. MMMMMnnn. (*Nodding.*)

BOBBY. Jerry, I hope ya don't mind us eatin' all your Devil Dogs. (*Jerry shakes his head.*)

GINNY. Maybe Catherine would like one.

BOBBY. Yeah? Would you like one?

CATHERINE. At this moment, I would like a Devil Dog more than anything else in the entire world.

BOBBY. (*Giving her one, takes another for himself.*) What the hell, I'll have another one.

47

STEVE. Why don't you have another one?

BOBBY. (*To himself.*) That's funny. (*Pause.*) Hey Stevie, guess what?

STEVE. What?

BOBBY. I'm gonna let ya ride shotgun.

STEVE. (*Dozing.*) You read my mind. (*Pause.*)

CATHERINE. Ginny, have you made up your mind?

GINNY. (*Looking back and forth from Jerry to Steve.*) Well . . . I . . . do you think I might have time for a little nap?

CATHERINE. (*Checking her watch.*) Oh sure. But we'll have to start very soon, so if you're coming with us—

GINNY. I just . . . really need to lie down for a few minutes. And then I'll see how I feel when I get up . . . I'm just so tired, I can't think straight. OK?

CATHERINE. That's fine. (*Catherine stretches out on the floor.*)

GINNY. Good. (*She starts off, then pauses and turns toward Jerry.*) I'm going to lie down for a few minutes. If you wanna change your mind—come with us—there's still time . . . (*Jerry doesn't answer.*) Stevie?

STEVE. (*Falling asleep.*) Hmmmmmn?

GINNY. (*She goes to Steve. Pauses.*) Someday I'm gonna let you take me to see *2001* in the movies. OK?

STEVE. (*Half asleep, but he's heard her.*) It's a date.

GINNY. Catherine—maybe you want to stretch out too.

CATHERINE. I think I will. (*She gets up. Looks at Bobby. He looks at her. She hands him the box of Devil Dogs.*) Don't eat all of those.

BOBBY. Hey. C'mon.

CATHERINE. You feel better?

BOBBY. Yeah . . . thanks. (*To Steve.*) Don't fall asleep on me, man.

STEVE. I just want to rest my eyes for a minute.

BOBBY. Didn't I tell ya' that was good smoke?

STEVE. Stays with you.

CATHERINE. Well, you have to know how to pace yourself. (*She joins Ginny in bedroom.*)

BOBBY. Hey Stevie . . . (*To Jerry.*) He's asleep.

JERRY. Yeah.

BOBBY. He was always a good sleeper.

JERRY. Listen. I'm sorry.

BOBBY. For what?

JERRY. Just I'm sorry.

48

BOBBY. Hey, ya don't have to be sorry. Ya got somethin' ya wanna say to me?

JERRY. Yeah.

BOBBY. Well?

JERRY. Shit!

BOBBY. Hey, c'mon.

JERRY. I don't know if I can make you understand.

BOBBY. Oh, I get ya.

JERRY. I didn't mean . . .

BOBBY. Sure. That's OK.

JERRY. When I was fired, walking around the streets? I thought of all the people I had worked with in the office.

BOBBY. Sure. Ya felt bad. I know.

JERRY. I could imagine them still at their desks, as if nothing had happened. As if nothing would ever happen. I knew I wasn't a part of their world. I knew it before they knew it. But I didn't know how to go back and say goodbye to them.

BOBBY. So ya didn't say anything.

JERRY. No.

BOBBY. Well . . . don't feel bad . . . it's over. Everything is gonna work out. You'll see. (*Jerry crosses to locker for his jacket and boots.*) Hey, where ya going?

JERRY. I have to get out.

BOBBY. What?

JERRY. I have to get some air. I want to get a little air.

BOBBY. Oh, sure. Quick walk around the block.

JERRY. Yeah. (*Jerry picks up paperback* Hamlet, *puts it in his pocket.*)

BOBBY. Yeah? . . . Do ya some good. Good idea. Gonna be nice out tonight, ya can tell. Fall's comin' . . . Is there anything special you want me to tell them when ya don't come back?

JERRY. (*He's been heading for the door. He stops.*) What?

BOBBY. Need some bucks?

JERRY. That's OK. I've got a little money I put aside.

BOBBY. 'Cause ya need it, I got the bread.

JERRY. (*He wants to go, but he can't.*) There's something I always meant to thank you for.

BOBBY. Me?

JERRY. That time in high school when I got into all that trouble.

BOBBY. Ya mean when ya ran away from home, and the cops caught up with ya in Delaware?

JERRY. And brought me home in a squad car. And my family

49

wouldn't speak to me, and all my friends, even Steve, were really hurt because I never told anyone I was going away, and . . .

BOBBY. Sure.

JERRY. You were the only one that didn't avoid me, or ask me why.

BOBBY. Yeah, well . . . shit. I figured ya do what ya think ya have to do.

JERRY. (*After a moment.*) Thank you. (*He leaves quickly. Bobby looks off after Jerry. He doesn't know what to do. He moves about the room, among the discarded remnants of the evening, looking and touching. Finally, he opens and shuts the locker door loudly enough so that Steve will wake up.*)

STEVE. (*Coming awake, but keeping his eyes closed.*) What?

BOBBY. Ya were snorin'.

STEVE. You woke me up to tell me I was snoring?

BOBBY. I was gonna wake ya up anyway. I wanna ask ya somethin'. Only ya gotta promise ya won't laugh.

STEVE. Hurry up. I'm falling asleep again.

BOBBY. OK. If I have to live on the moon someday, would ya visit me? Don't laugh . . . Well?

STEVE. Only if you have a television.

BOBBY. (*Smiling.*) That's what I love about ya, Stevie.

STEVE. What?

BOBBY. Ya never change. (*As Bobby moves away Upstage, lights fade, until only Steve's face is lit. He stares straight ahead.*)

FADEOUT

AUTHOR'S NOTE

Say Goodnight, Gracie was originally performed without an intermission. I believed that the play was better served without a break of any kind, and I have had no reason to think otherwise.

However, if an intermission is going to be used, I would recommend that it come right before Catherine's big speech on the Cuban Missile Crisis. The last line and direction for Act I would be:

BOBBY. Thanks. (*No one moves. It should be clear that they're all very stoned.*)

FADEOUT

Act II would open with everyone in the same positions. Catherine would begin her speech.

COSTUME NOTE

Steve's gorilla mask should somehow be a cross between the masks used in *Planet of the Apes* and *2001*. There should be holes for the actor's eyes; the mask should not be too rigid; nor should it be hideous-looking. Anyone who can obtain a photograph, or view a videotape of Ernie Kovacs' Nairobi Trio will understand.

PROPERTY PLOT

Offstage: (by character)

JERRY: Shoulder strap carry-all bag with books (lg. sect.) 8×10 headshot with resumé (middle sect.) key ring with keys (front sect.).

STEVE: Gorilla mask, derby hat, "Marlboro" pack with several cigarettes, matches.

GINNY: Bicentennial cleaning bag over dress.

BOBBY: "Marlboro" pack with several cigarettes, matches.

CATHERINE: "Stash" box with at least 3 joints, lighter.

Onstage: preset

Lockers: (C.R.)

    D.: Shelf: "Hamlet" paperback (U. side). "Pepto Bismol" bottle (D. side). U. Rear Hook: pea jacket.

    U.: D. Front Hook: spring exerciser. Floor: pair barbells (front), exercise mat (rolled up on end) (rear).

Television: (D.R.)

    D.R. edge: silver plastic ashtray with matches.

    R. of TV on floor: black desk phone.

Below Loft: (U.)

    On hook D.L.: "Ginny's" blue jeans with belt.

    Floor U.L.: "Ginny's" loafers with blue knee socks.

Sofa: (C.)

    R. sect.: C.: gold sachet pillow leaning on back. L.: red satin heart pillow leaning on back.

    L. sect.: draped by black print fabric—border diagonal C. to L.

    S,R.: cowboy print pillow leaning on back. C.: beige pillow leaning on back. L.: abstract print pillow leaning on back.

Coffee Table (wooden cable spool): (D.C.)

    Top: *plate* with coffee mug, fork, leftover toast, and egg yolk painted on; bit of coffee, pencil—D.L.; horn—C.; aviator sunglasses—U.C.

    Shelf Below: R.: gumball machine (toy, plastic) C.: book ("At The Feet Of the Master") L.: pink ceramic vase, with little girl sculpted on front.

Radiator: (D.L.)

    folding chair leaning on it (onstage side) upholstered side facing onstage.

Armchair: (C.L.)

    D.—stuffed black cat facing R. Copy of "Backstage" under cat's paws. Ashtray with matches at front corner of chair.

Bathtub: (U.L.)

"polaroid" camera (no film) D. side.

Sink: (U.L.)

saucepan with handle facing D. (U. side)

Refrigerator: (U.L.C.)

2 cans of Beer ("Bud") on door shelf. 32 oz. diet 7up bottle (filled with water) centre top shelf and filler.

Kitchen Cabinet: (U.C.)

Top Shelf: R.: soup cans. L.: filler.

Middle Shelf: R.: incense, incense burner, matches. Front: ashtray. L.: at least 5 glasses.

Bottom Shelf: R.: full box "Devil Dogs." C.: roll of paper towels. L.: metal tray standing on end.

COSTUME PLOT

JERRY:
   Blue-grey-white tattersall plaid sports jacket
   Blue and white, long sleeved, striped shirt
   Navy blue tie
   Dark blue tee shirt, short sleeved
   Navy blue, corduroy, jean-styled slacks
   Grey leather belt
   Blue socks
   Black short leather boots
   Navy pea coat

STEVE:
   Tan wide-wale corduroy sports jacket with elbow patches (lt. brn.)
   Pink and white stripe madras cotton long-sleeved shirt
   Maroon bow tie
   Tan cotton chino type slacks with cuffs
   Tan web belt
   White short tube socks
   Tan suede rubber soled shoes
   School ring

BOBBY:
   Light blue denim colored snap-front shirt with rust edged double ruffle
      front
   Rust suede open front vest with 2 front pockets (patch)
   Light blue denim straight legged jeans
   Brown braided leather belt
   White short tube socks
   Rust short leather boots
   Gold colored crucifix on gold colored chain
   Multi-toned brown suede patch overcoat with cuffs

GINNY:
   Tan leather slip ons (shoes)
   Tan cotton wrap skirt
   Pantyhose
   Navy and light brown suede and crocheted vest
   Maroon long-sleeved small collared overblouse
   Dark blue jeans (preset on stage)*
   Navy blue kneehigh socks (preset on stage)*
   Cordovan loafers (preset on stage)*
   White plastic heart on gold colored neck chain
   Medium brown suede jacket
   Brown leather shoulder bag purse

CATHERINE:
  Purple jersey halter dress with waist sash
  Pantyhose
  Off-white dress shoes
  Chain and stone necklace with stone pendant
  Purple velvet evening bag with gold chain shoulderstrap
  Peach and gold colored crocheted shawl with fringe
  Watch
  Solid bangle bracelet 1" wide gold color
  Gold hoop earrings

SOUND PLOT

Hot-wire telephone: onstage—wired to switch operated offstage.

Door buzzer: practical—on u. edge of door frame with buzzer attached to set u. wall.

AUTHOR'S NOTES

In November, 1982, *Say Goodnight, Gracie* was taped for airing on WTTW, the PBS television station in Chicago. The exigencies of that taping, requiring that the play not run over 90 minutes, resulted in the director (Austin Pendleton) and myself taking red pencils to the text one last time to determine what might be most judiciously "lost." Some of the subsequent cuts proved so effective in performance that I have chosen to list them here. Anyone directing future productions of *Gracie* is therefore advised to make the following deletions:

p. 9   Cut from STEVE'S "Are you all right?" near top of page all the way to the bottom.

p. 10   Cut from top of page to STEVE'S "Because I'm your friend" several lines down.

(This new sequence now reads as follows: After JERRY'S line, "Do you agree?" on top of p. 9, we cut all the way to STEVE'S "What's the matter?" Did your boss give you more static about taking off to go to auditions?" on p. 10.)

p. 14   Top: Cut from JERRY'S "Why do you love to make up stories about me?" all the way to his ". . . my relationship with Ginny is one of them."

        Bottom: Cut JERRY'S last bit of dialogue, from "Look, I'm sorry" to "Please understand that."

p. 15   Top: Cut GINNY'S line: "Besides, it's *your* reunion, not *mine!*

        Middle: Cut GINNY'S lines: "How am I supposed to entertain your friends if you won't help me? Or don't you care if anyone feels welcome in our home anymore? Answer me Jerry!"

p. 33 Cut from CATHERINE'S "I don't think the subject ever came up before, Bobby." to the end of BOBBY'S ". . . gonna pull the plug on our livin' together."

p. 34 Cut from STEVE'S "Ralph Kramden coming home from work and finding Alice in bed with Ed Norton" to JERRY'S "Excuse me, Steve" several lines down.

(This new sequence reads as follows: After the end of CATHERINE'S speech at top of page ". . . and, really, what could be more exciting than that?" the next line is JERRY'S "You know what I think is really exciting?")

p. 39 Within STEVE'S second exchange of dialogue near top of page, cut from "Has anybody ever met Jerry's boss?" to the end.

Bottom: Cut from BOBBY'S "Jerry, I'm sorry ya lost your job" to JERRY'S "What?"

(This new sequence reads as follows: After JERRY'S "It was just a part-time job—a survival job—it wasn't important—" the next line is STEVE'S "Thanks a lot for confiding in me, by the way.")

p. 40 Cut from top of page to end of JERRY'S line, "He said I'd been taking off too often to go to auditions."

The next section, beginning with CATHERINE'S "Did you want to get fired?" to BOBBY'S "She thinks she's a doctor" should be retained as it appears. Everything else on this page should be cut, with the exception of the last line, BOBBY'S "Ginny, what's the matter?"

(This new sequence should play as indicated below)

BOBBY. (*To the group.*) She thinks she's a doctor. (*To Ginny.*) Ginny, what's the matter?

p. 44 Middle: CATHERINE'S speech should be cut so that it plays as indicated below:

57

CATHERINE. Of course not. It's just like this very brilliant psychologist, whose name escapes me at the moment, but whom I usually have dinner with whenever I'm on stopover in Paris, is writing a book about Contemporary Manifestations of —

BOBBY. (*Cutting her off.*) Boy, am I ever sick of hearin' about this fuckin' doctor!

—Ralph Pape
January, 1983

New

TITLES

A WALK IN THE WOODS
BURN THIS
THE BOYS NEXT DOOR
GUS AND AL
HEATHEN VALLEY
AMERICAN NOTES
EVENING STAR
SHOOTING STARS
MAX AND MAXIE
YEAR OF THE DUCK
THE JOHNSTOWN VINDICATOR
A GRAND ROMANCE
ONE THING MORE
THE ROAD TO THE GRAVEYARD
CROSSIN' THE LINE

● *Write for Information*

DRAMATISTS PLAY SERVICE, INC.

440 Park Avenue South   New York, N.Y. 10016